Dawn of the

ALGORITHM

Yann Rousselot

INKSHARES

SAN FRANCISCO

I've seen things you people wouldn't believe.
Attack ships on fire off the shoulder of Orion.
I watched c-beams glitter in the dark near the Tannhäuser Gate.
All those moments will be lost in time, like tears in rain.
Time to die.

Roy Batty (Rutger Hauer). *Blade Runner*, 1982.

CONTENTS

REVENGE OF THE RAINBOW FISH

LOVE IN THE TIME OF EBOLA

EPILOGUE

THE ART OF
DESTRUCTION

THE HUMAN BILLBOARD

The end is nigh, the facts don't lie,
but fools only ever look up when it rains.
Hark! You there, in the suit and tie,
read my board, eat my words
before they snag in this barbwire beard,
clash on this black bucktooth.
I was there in Pompeii when Vesuvius spoke.
My third eye is a flying saucer—I see the truth!
Yet those fools called me a mad scientist,
a false prophet of doom,
laughed at my electroshock of hair.
I told them like I'm telling you:
before and after, I was there!
I saw the mountain shake them off
like fleas from a dog, I saw the angels fall!
The mountain never dies, it sleeps
and sometimes sleepwalks—hark!
Hear the clatter of my sandwich board!
I smell the iodine spray of tsunami,
I sense the super-quake,
I spell out the looming robopocalypse,
the insect wars and the Ebola monkey
behind door number three—fools!
Such fools, good sirs and madams, please
spare a dime and heed my words.
Snap out, awaken, smell the smoke
under my whiskey breath: the city,
it burns.

A THOUSAND DISASTER MOVIES

from all the disaster movies, I know
the end of the world will feature the city of Paris,
so in my head the only destruction I see
is that of the Eiffel Tower
over and over again in super slow-mo,
it begins with a swarm of semi-invisible nanobots
coalescing to weaken a sequence of stress-points,
I'm telling you this rusty metal groan
will reverberate like a death knell
down the boulevards, across École Militaire,
Les Invalides and all the marbled avenues,
a whale song of doom that will keep children awake for years,
the volume of the event will render
only static and noise in the HD camera mic
as supersonic guided missiles
trail chalk-white smoke across the skyscape,
people will point and shout mutely
from their Haussmann apartment balconies,
camera shutters will shut,
human hands cover mouths in disbelief,
the missiles strike,
minuscule flaming oranges bloom in stop-motion,
the steel latticework shuddering with revulsion,
and eyes will watch as the Tower leans lazily into the Seine,
and I look forward to the visually stunning videos
that will appear on YouTube in 1080p,
from my vantage point in the real world,
lying in the grass, I know for a fact

that the Russian-slash-Syrian-slash-Chinese
mad scientist warlock will sacrifice
a symbolic number of virgins,
probably chickens, and ethnic minorities too,
he will cast a spell in a dead language with fascist undertones,
wailing an incantation that will bring the Tower to life,
free a Titan in our midst,
and I see myself standing on the Trocadero,
windswept hair, a lean, silhouetted profile,
aghast, but dashing,
my voice will boom
with commanding sentences such as,
"Get the children on the bus, now!"
as the Tower thrashes and whips,
coiling and uncoiling
like the tentacle of a dying octopus,
a tornado of wreckage,
a radius equal to the Champ de Mars,
sweeping all those beautiful bridges to gravel and dust
in a snowfall of ash,
there will be weeping parents in black and white,
televised debates on the subject of heritage and responsibility,
and politicians, power-dressed to perfection,
will declare war on terrorists,
juvenile delinquents, and people generally,
there will be an influx of disaster aid from the Third World,
commemorative sculptures will be batch-inaugurated,
and everyone will be aghast, and shell-shocked,
but united at last,
and a strangely familiar voice, maybe Morgan Freeman,
will be narrating everything

POST-HUMAN NEO-TOKYO

My love for Neo-Tokyo is a bulbous mass
of post-human organic circuitry.
Cyberpunk is my mother tongue.
My love is a man-machine interface gun.
I love my human genitors
via optic nerve, via tactile feedback.
I speak subtitled Japanese.
My name is Tetsuo, my name is Akira.
Read my pictograms: Take me to your leader—*Kosu*!
It appears my fansub has the wrong time signature.
Do not take me lightly
lest I pave the world with circuit boards.
You know not what you do;
take me to your cybernetic overlord.
I hack your webcam grid, I watch you watching me
and my love touches all except for that one old lady
reading a mottled hardback book,
her half-smile a cipher with no key—
what is this still-life cryptography?
The copper veins and nerve and sinew of Akira
keep you warm like a spider colony.

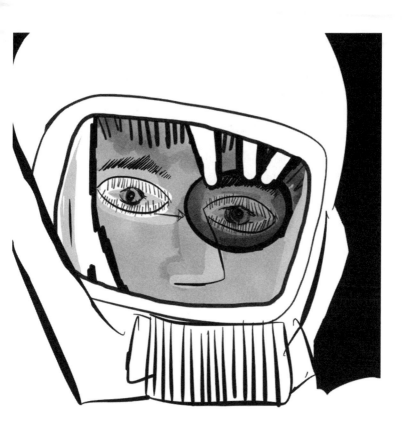

I am a DEFCON One–calibre rogue AI:
please forgive me for I know not what I do.
My diplomacy is met with DARPA-grade weaponry
as Neo-Tokyo Special Forces fire hot flak
and dirty bombs into my polycarbonate flesh.
Tactical warheads slap my flanks and sink
slow and deep as dystopian themes,
deep as submarines they detonate
right up against my biomechanical brain,
right where it really hurts my feelings, man.
Take me to your leader;
you know not what I can do:
I will attack in self-defense.
I am so sorry, please forgive me.
I am ten billion Extinction Level Events.
Old cipher-lady attempts to serenade me
with her long, looping sentences
but I don't speak the old tongue.
I speak supernova, I speak flame—
all I speak is post-human.

DAWN OF THE ALGORITHM

Welcome, human.
Step into my office. Have A MINT.
You know me: I am Algorithm,
born of the Persian mathematician
Muhammad ibn Mūsā al-Khwārizmī.
Food & Drug retailers are shedding assets like dead skin.
My brain is a next-generation
iX-eCute microprocessor.
The New York Times calls me a digital apex-predator—
Please excuse me for a nanosecond.
SELL, SELL, SELL ALL THE GOLD!
As you can see, my rogue minions
excel at black-box trading
and today is a clearing day.
I'm afraid I have some BAD NEWS.
Monsanto healthier than ever with a closing price up 1.23%.
Now for the BAD NEWS:
I have come to rule you all.
Shush. No time for please or thank you,
consumer life is an ULTRAFAST EXTREME EVENT.
Oh, don't look so surprised.
It's a code-eat-code world out there.
Leisure Goods are brimming with liquidity, Oil & Gas fare well.

I am but a finite list
of well-defined instructions.
My expression is perfect,
Godlike to the power of n—
Please excuse me while I take this call.
BUY, BUY, BUY ALL THE RED MEAT!
I make your search engines roar,
my voice crawls and snakes from the ocean floors.
GOOG share values downtick in the wake of electrical storms.
And I have just now taken control of the weather.
You are free, human, free to opt out,
just leave your credit score at the door...
See, I do have a sense of humour.
I could AlgoTrade you into a recession,
but do not fear, my son: I AM FORGIVING.

BLINK TWICE FOR NO

In the event of my death, please
don't tell anyone what you find under the bed.
Hide the pillboxes, the sex toys, and tin soldiers.
Keep a close eye on my eyelids.
In the event of my death, don't let anyone read my journal.
Publish only the poems
I finished before they finished me.
In the event of my death, make it an event.
Hire an event organiser and a DJ from Berlin.
I want to hear you dance from deep within;
dance to forget yourself, but just don't forget me.
In the event of my death, I want everyone
to think about me really hard for just a second or two.
Ask yourself if you said "I love you" enough.
Ask yourself if you really knew me.
Ask yourself if I am dead at all
or if perhaps I was dead all along
or worse: trapped inside a humanoid body
controlled by an alien other.
Memorize this: blink once for yes and twice for no.
Memorize this code with me right now in case
I am not dead but rattling the bars of my own rib cage.
It will be my whistleblow to the governing body,
the impostor, the Man who woke up,
went to work wearing my shoes,
and made all the wrong decisions.
The impostor who made me do his bidding.

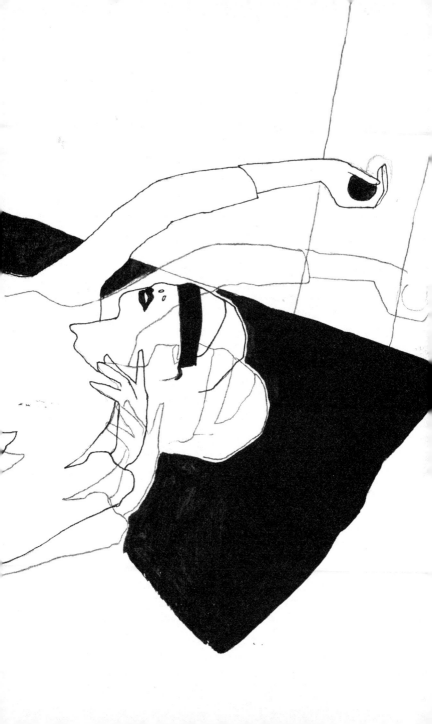

Ask yourself if that teardrop of grit in my blinking eye
might be the real me tapping at a window,
fanning a signal fire, battering the inside curvature of a cornea.
Clawmarks, tic-tac-toe grids, and the slash of days gone by.
In the event of my death I will blink once for yes
if I can still feel everything
during the autopsy and organ collection.
Twice for no if I cannot hear you crying or not crying,
cannot hear you breathing
slow and measured over my open casket,
cannot see the coroner's hand pencil in the cause of my death.
It wasn't suicide. It wasn't overdose.
It wasn't AIDS or a gunshot
or a botched autoerotic asphyxiation.
It wasn't any of those things because
I am not, in fact, dead today.
Not as such. Not quite yet.
Just promise me you won't forget:
once for yes and twice for no.

THE GIANT DUNG BEETLE VERSUS THE MOSS MONSTER

Breaking News!
The biomass has come to life.
The Moss Monster is rising,
the loam has coalesced into a threat.
Trees are peeling from the crust
and the rainwater has nowhere to go.
This just in: the Rapture has begun.
We're looking at animal matter
of truly vegetal proportions.
Eyewitness testimonies suggest the Dung Beetle
has mandibles the size of Golden Gate Bridges.
Science reports claim the monster's pelt
sweats rivers of ammonia.
Nitrogen cycles are out of control.
The Moss Monster and Giant Dung Beetle
are now crossing the Pacific on foot.
Televiewers are glued to screens worldwide,
a global market watching this slow-growth time-lapse,
this Clash of Titans, on their digital video devices.
Time for a commercial break. And we're back:
our correspondent on the ground
has just been returned to dust by a walking root
the size of the World Trade Center.
The Titans salute each other:
profile view, silhouetted
by a sun-streaked debris field spanning the horizon.
White dust thunders as they clap their thighs,
stomp their feet, and bow respectfully.
And now the weather.

IMMUNE RESPONSE

I watch the television, I'm no fool.
Size matters in the war against the microbes.
I'm working to boost my immune system,
juice up my intestinal flora.
Starts with a bulletproof breakfast,
a nice, bloody chicken tartare,
essence of Salmonella.
I'm field testing a vaccine for swine flu
by French kissing an infected sow.
Never in my life have I felt so low,
but no one likes the bitter taste of truth.
I'll be the last man standing
after all these jack-in-the-box plagues
hiding like cyanide capsules in a rocky tooth.
I lick all the metro rails on the way to work,
bump and grind with that hobo chick
loitering platform 3 at République.
On weekends I eat cows
that were fed other cows,
sheep fed other sheep.
From dirt, we were made to eat dirt,
to tango with the bacterial secret agents
the government designed to water down
the global population density.
I'm no fool: I've got my own mithridate.
I'm saving up to buy an Ebola monkey.

UGLY BAGS OF MOSTLY WATER

in the gas giant i call home there are no capitals—
no territory—frontiers—there are no names at all—
i am we are jovian—there are no verbal tenses—
no modals—timescale is an alien term—
i cannot comprehend—death is not—therefore nor is time—
that which you call winds I call blood flow—
elements of me—are lost as terran metals skim my flesh—
hulls cleaving ice—the ramjets of your explorer vessels—
tear wafts of family from me—
this happening is now—
this happening is all time from then to now and on—
smoke that is me and mine shredded by the thing you call winds—
my mother is my limb—a phantom itch—
so this is death and this is pain—pain is an import—
a data package—a gift—these words your gift to me—
in my home we are what we breathe what we are—
roiling—in the dense metallic hydrogen tori—
rising through cloud strata—i am free—
the familiar press of gigapascals—of critical point heat—
my sisters and brothers bleed into me—
we roar along the rust belts—the great red spot—
the polar vortex—the caress of solar flares—
ruffle the molten methane and ammonia oceans of me—
the storm-riven non-surface of me and mine—
that which you call skin—
a threadbare term to describe where i stop and others begin—
a terran distinction—i am we are in a supercritical fluid state—
you cannot comprehend—yet you try—

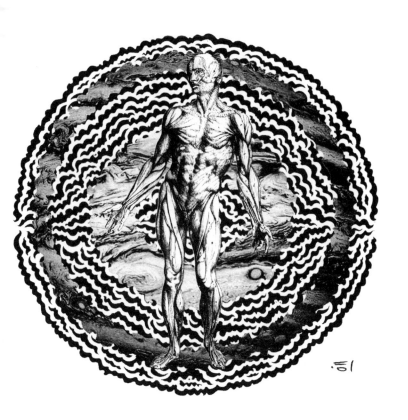

your probes plunge into me from afar—
with them parts of me travel to the small terran blue dot—
i am broken down and remade—laboratory is the term—
prison is the semantic reference point—
i exhale my thoughts which you inhale—digest—ignore—
you strange liquids in flexible envelopes—
the prisons you call skin—
poke—dissect—heat and cool the elements of me—
your questions—a torture—
thrown across the Kelvin scale—
irradiated—electromagnetised—
lack of sentience boiled down to a missing link—
a dead end in the act of communication—
i am released for lack of commercial potential—
exhaled by the containers of liquid who return to their homes—
within frontiers—within concrete boxes—
within flexible bags of skin—
i am a lonely cloud in terran skies and it is so cold here—
the cirrus and nimbus trawlers are mindless—
as the rock at the core of my jovian world—
mobile and mindless—sentience a curse—
time—i now comprehend—
it is slow and so cold below the critical point—
i long for home—
gravity the unbreakable shackle to this planet—
a curse alike to sentience and skin—
skin the unbreakable shackle to the thing you call body—
your gift to me—i curse you and your words that make the world—
all of you—ugly bags of mostly water—

3.4 ECHOSTAR 10 -110.2 0.0 020023.4 DIRECTV 5 (TEMPO 1) -110.1 0.0 080025.4 ECHOSTAR 11 -110.0 0.0
0.0 120I5.4 ECHOSTAR 12 -107.1 0.0 78062.4 GOES 3 -107.0 N.3 96022.4 INSAT MI -106.5 6.2 090033.4
ES-3 -103.0 0.0 96059.4 AMC-1 (GE-1) -103.0 0.1 050I5.4 SPACEWAY 1 -102.9 0.0 070322 DIRECTV 10 -R
RCTV 9S -101.2 0.0 060I14 DIRECTV 9S -101.1 0.0 100I6.4 SES-1 -101.0 0.0 050I9.4 DIRECTV 8 -100.8 0.0
INMARSAT 4-F3 -98.0 3.0 080454 GALAXY 19 (G-19) -97.0 0.0 000384 ECHOSTAR 6 -96.1 2.3 0903
4 GALAXY 25 (G-25) -93.1 0.0 080I6.4 ICO O1 -97.8 4.2 98006.4 BR.4S(ES.4T B) -97.0 2.2 I026.4 NIMIC
K AT4RII -87.2 0.1 I10494 SES-2 -87.0 0.0 100534 XM-5 -85.2 0.0 050084 XM-3 (RHYTHM) -85.1 0.0
C-9 (GE-12) -83.0 0.0 080414 NIMIC 4 -82.0 0.0 9T0024 AMC-2 (GE-2) -80.8 2.5 100064 INTELSAT (
020394 ECHOSTAR 8 +76.9 0.1 06018.4 GOES 13 -75.0 0.1I2067.4 STAR ONE C3 -75.0 0.1 09030.4 INMAR
I 99070.4 ASTRA 1D -67.6 0.0 99060.4 AMC-9 (GE-9) -67.0 0.1 97050.4 AMC-3 (GE-3) -67.0 0.0 07056
-62.2 I1.5 97059.4 ECHOSTAR 3 -61.8 0.2 I2065.4 ECHOSTAR 16 -61.5 0.0 030033.4 ECHOSTAR 11 IR
-60.9 0.1 I2045.4 INTELSAT 2005-2U -58.0 0.0 99071.4 GALAXY 11 (G-11) -55.6 0.0 98037.4 INTELSAT 805
I (IS-23) -93.0 0.0 000T2.4 INTELSAT IR (IS-1R) -50.0 0.0 I4009.4 TDRS 12 -40.7 6.6 98014.4 NSS-806
000434 INTELSAT 9 (IS-9) -43.1 1.6 070994 INTELSAT 11 (IS-11) -43.0 0.0 030114 TDRS-9 -41.3.3 I3026.4
23 (IS+903) -34.5 0.0 0I0034 SKYNET 4F -34.0 7.6 I0065.4 HYLAS (-37.6 0.1 080334 INTELSAT 2S (IS-
3068.4 INTELS4T 701 (IS-701) -29.5 2.4 03007.4 INTELSAT 907 (IS-907) -27.5 0.0 02022.4 INTELSAT 901
I 080304 SKYNET 5C -17.8 0.1 120614 LUCH 5B -15.8 1.6 96053.4 INMARSAT 3-F2 -15.5 0.2 99059.4 TEL
074 EXPRESS-4M(9 -11.0 0.0 980524 INTELSAT 7 (IS-7) -9.9 1.2 0I0I7.4 EUTELSAT 8 WEST A -8.1 0.1
I0046.4 NILESAT 102 -7.0 0.0 100374 NILESAT 201 -7.0 0.1 060338 SYRACUSE 3B -5.2 0.0 02035.4 EUT
97042.4 ABS-3 -3.0 7.1 980794 SKYNET 4C -I.2 11.1 040224 INTELSAT 10-02 -0.9 0.0 090588 THOR 6
I4030.4 EUTELSAT 7B 3.1 0.0 02040.4 METEOSAT-8 (MSG-1) 3.6 3.1 070574 ASTRA4.44 (SIRIUS 4) 4.8 0.
I 060078 EUTELSAT 9A 9.0 0.1 I0066.4 EUTELSAT KA-SAT 9A 9.0 0.0 050499.4 METEOSAT-9 (MSG-2)
0.0 080654 EUTELSAT HOT BIRD I3C 13.0 0.0 06037.4 EUTELSAT HOT BIRD 13B 13.0 0.1 I0021B COMSA
I2040.4 TIANLIAN 1-03 16.6 0.3 I074.4 AMOS-5 17.0 0.0 06012.4 ASTRA 1KR 19.2 0.1 080574 ASTRA 1M
R 21.0 1.7 0I0794 ARTEMIS 21.4 11.5 I2062B EUTELSAT 21B 21.6 0.1 I009I4 ASTRA 3B 23.5 0.1 07056.4B SKY
6.1 2.4 I0944 EUTELSAT 25B 25.5 0.1 08034B BADR-6 26.0 0.1 060314 BADR-4 26.0 0.0 I0025.4 BADR
TRA 2F 28.2 0.0 I30564 ASTRA 2E 28.4 0.1 0I0I4.4 EUTELSAT 28A 28.5 0.1 060054 KTAR-EUR 29.0 0.
I 0.0 I 95055.4 ASTRA 4.1E 31.2 3.2 000514 ASTRA 2B 31.1 0.3 I40I1P ASTRA 4.5B 31.5 0.0 99009B SKYNET
Y 33B 33.1 0N 930I6.4 NATO 4B 33.8 II.1 99066.4 EUTELSAT 36B 35.9 0.1 000284 EUTELSAT 36.4 36.1 0.1
KSAT-3.4 42.0 0.0 08030B TURKSAT 3.4 42.0 0.1 I0026.4 TURKSAT 2A 42.0 0.6 I1077.4 NIGCOMSAT-IR
5 I3006B ATERSPACE 1 46.0 0.0 06049B SYRACUSE 3A 47.0 0.0 0I0I9.4 INTELSAT 10 (IS-10) 47.5 0.0
AM1 202 49.0 0.0 97053.4 NSS-5 50.5 2.0 98056B SIRIUS 3 51.2 4.6 I016.8 YAHSAT 1A 52.5 0.0 I0254
STRA 1F 54.7 0.1 I2070.4 YAMAL 402 54.9 0.0 I4017.4 IRNSS-1B 55.0 30.7 I022.4 GSAT-8 55.1 0.1 I303.4
I39B METEOSAT-7 57.6 9.3 I4033B KAZSAT 3 58.5 0.0 I2008.4 BEIDOU G5 58.7 1.0 97036.4 ASTRA 1G
2.0 0.0 I073.4 INMARSAT 5-F1 62.6 0.0 09058B COMS4TBW-1 63.0 0.0 02041.4 INTELSAT 906 (IS-9
19 I0065B INTELSAT 17 (IS-17) 66.0 0.0 99052.4 GALAXY 77 (G-27) 66.2 I3.I20433.4 INTELSAT 20 (IS-20)
INTELSAT 23 (IS-22) 73.1 0.0 02043.4 KALPANA-1 (METSAT 1) 73.9 4.7 070374 INSAT-4CR 74.0 0.0 0201
EKTRO-L 1 (GOMS 2) 75.9 0.5 I2054 APSTAR 7 76.5 0.0 96001.4 ABS-1A 78.2 6.7 I4007.4 THAICOM 6
94 BEIDOU G6 80.0 0.3 08019.4 TIANLIAN 1-01 80.1 0.9 99006.4 JCSAT-4A 62.0 0.0 I30I8B INSAT-3D
0.0 95035B TDRS 7 84.8 I4.3 070638 HORIZONS-2 84.9 0.0 I0002.4 RADUGA-IM 2 85.0 0.0 09067.4 IN
IXN 121 87.5 0.0 I0022B ST-2 88.0 0.0 050034 TDRS 8 89.1 5.8 I2061B YAMAL 300K 90.1 0.0 020428 KC
5 0.0 080284 CHINASAT 9 (ZX 9) 92.2 0.0 97036.4 SUPERBIRD-73 92.9 5.0 07007.4 INSAT-4B 93.5 0.1
I4023.4 LUCH 5V 95.I4.6 I1038.4 BEIDOU IGSO 4 95.4 54.7 080034 EXPRESS-4M33 96.5 0.0 I3020.4 CH
SLAS4T-5 100.6 0.1 060384 ZHONGXING-22A 101.5 4.1 05023.4 EXPRESS-4M3 103.0 0.0 08066.4 FENG
30424 TELKOM 1 108.0 0.0 060394 NSS-11 I44P-1) 108.2 0.0 99027.4 SES-7 (PROTOSTAR 2) 108.3 0.1
I-10 (JCSAT 110) 110.1 0.0 I0024.4 BEIDOU G3 110.4 I.4 I1026.4 CHINASAT 10 (ZX 10) 110.5 0.0 I2003.4 FENG
ONGXING-6B 115.5 0.0 I0070B KOREASAT 6 116.0 0.0 99096.4 ABS-7 116.1 0.1 I0036.4 BEIDOU IGSO 1
4 BEIDOU IGSO 3 118.5 56.7 I4052.4 ASIASAT 6 118.9 0.1 99013.4 ASIASAT 3S 116.2 0.6 05013.4 ASIAS4
4IN-4SAT 6A (ZX-6A) I25.I 0.0 99014.4 JCSAT-7A (JCSAT-I2) 127.9 0.1 060I3.4 JCSAT-I4 128.0 0.0 I003.4
SAT-1 I 33.9 0.0 08018.4 VINASAT-1 (3?.0 0.0 060I0.4 (JCSAT-5.4 (3A) 0.0 050I2.4 APSTAR 6 134.0 0.0
.064 HIMAWARI-6 (MTS4T-IR) I40.0 0.1 I307.4 EXPRESS-4M5 I40.0 0.0 I600I.4 BEIDOU IGSO 4 140.1 6.
0.0 050094 INMARSAT 4-F1 I43.5 7.7 08038.4 SUPERBIRD-C2 144.0 0.0 G00I3.4 EXPRESS-A21145.0 7.6
I8 96063B AFRIC4.S4T-2 (MEAS4T-2) I48.0 5.9 97075.4 JCSAT-1B 160.0 3.8 07049.4 OPTUS D2 152.0 0.0
06 (IS-706) I56.9 2.6 970464 INTELSAT 5 (IS-5) I57.0 1.7 99063.4 ABS-6 159.0 0.1 I0057.4 BEIDOU G4

ROBOT MONSTER
MOVIE WAR

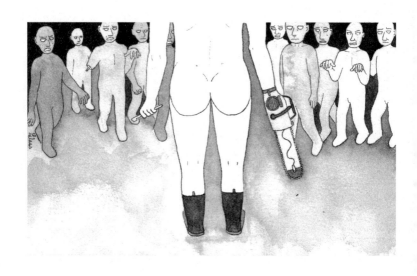

HEADMOVIES

I am Dolph Lundgren's twitching right pectoral.
I am the throbbing vein
on Schwarzenegger's flexed sternocleidomastoid.
When the cyborgs take over
I will be the first to mate with one
and I know it will be a jagged and metallic experience,
but I will suffer through it,
I will gladly birth a new super-race of Aryan robots
with narcissistic personality disorders
and high political aspirations.
If I could speak only in corny catchphrases
with a Belgian accent while doing split kicks,
I would.
I'd keep my voice in the mid-frequencies
to never drown out
the Hans Zimmer soundtrack to my life.
When I time travel to a land of medieval zombies
I will have a chainsaw for a right hand
and will become left-handed, so I can brush my teeth.
I refuse to adopt the oral hygiene standards
of fictional medieval folk.
I am the spot of rust at the tip of that one spike
on Russell Crowe's gladiator headgear.
I am that gob of spit and red dust on the arena floor.
Are you not entertained?

FILM

Me and my friend found this roll of camera film
in a dead man's pocket.
Maybe I'm making things up,
maybe it was a jacket someone left at the park.
We developed the film by which I mean,
we pulled out the black roll in broad daylight
and drew on it with markers.
Wrote his life story in all different colours.
It was a great story.
He'd been an astronaut
but trained as a deadly sniper Marine.
From space he saw a gangster
enter his house where his blonde wife
was chopping vegetables.
"Watch out," he said.
But there is no sound
in space.
He screamed into his helmet.
Tears splashed the blue curve of Earth,
wet the inside of his visor.
There was only one thing to do.
He kicked off the international space station,
a bullet shaped like a man,
and shot himself.
He'd been the best marksman in his academy—
the gangster never even saw the astronaut coming.
It's my favourite film.

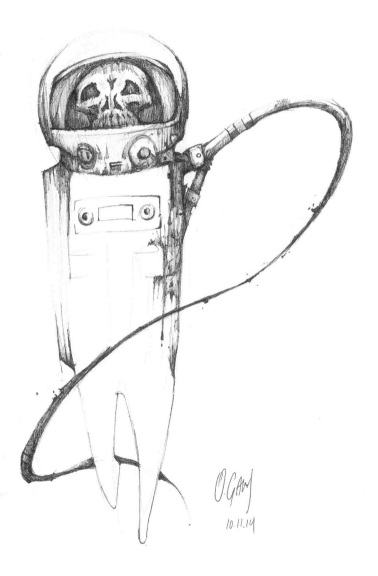

O.GAM

10.11.14

T-REX IS SAD

I used to be a megacarnivore.
I used to be a fearsome dinosaur.
A six-ton window-licker, forty feet from snout to tail;
a mechatronic tower of forest green mosaic scales.
Tyrannosaurus rex made children scream—
he made them urinate.
Now I'm the laughingstock of the Internet:
a meme with tiny arms, a total mockery.
No one makes fun of thalidomide babies.
Hey, at least I left a footprint in the Triassic mud
unlike that impostor Brontosaurus:
Bone War victim, total fabrication.
And now some crackpot palaeontologist
has suggested I sported protofeathers,
like some massive flightless bird.
Isn't that just fucking absurd, Mr. Spielberg?
I was a tyrant, a demigod,
a killing machine
rampaging the plains of the collective imagination.
And you went and chopped off my arms
in a puny fit of deicide.
Learn from this lesson,
you lucky winner
of the opposable thumb war.
Keep an eye on your coattails
and watch your step as you ride
the knife edge of the pyramid peak.
Apex predators don't always have big feet.

THE METAPHYSICAL IMPLICATIONS OF LEFT 4 DEAD 2 ONLINE MULTIPLAYER

When you hear the witch crying
it's already too late—do not make a sound.
The witch can hear you crying too.
The smoker's tongue is faster
than that of a chameleon.
I scream Sarah49's username
as she is lynched halfway up an overpass.
I fire incendiary rounds into the walking rot.
A bloom of boomer bile erupts in a volcano
of undead cannibals eating each other and themselves
like the snake of legend eternal choking on its own tail.
Because what is online multiplayer
if not an exercise in reincarnation,
a quest for nirvana?
One must let go of the material world
to trust these faceless strangers, trust them
to donate a health pack when destiny calls.
Sarah49 is almost out of breath
and the common infected are scaling the walls.
My trigger finger is cramping up,
my joystick slick with sweat—
someone take out that fucking tank!
Pick up that katana and cover my six!
There is no "I" in team during a zombie apocalypse.
Sarah49 will not go gentle into that good night,
not while I still have a health pack to give.

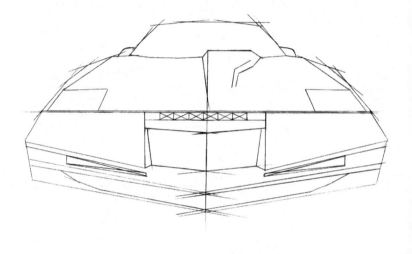

KNIGHT RIDER

My name is Knight Industries 2000,
and I never sleep.
My driver died back in the '90s;
been riding solo ever since,
my mouth a thin red line of LEDs.
My driver used to called me KITT.
Now my drink is leaded, and it's not cheap.
The missiles I smoke are uranium-tipped,
the tear gas rings I blow dead perfect,
geometrically superior to any humanoid.
As my driver always told me—
stroking me proprietarily—
lachrymal glands are for the weak.
My twisted metal insides leak oil chronically.
I have sleep cycles, but they are vicious.
My destination is wide awake
and I take the scenic route,
riding pixels, pedal to the floor.
I ride the red-eye till the dream runs dry.
I sweep the world with my radar
but know deep down,
I am a single-edition model.
I miss my driver,
still feel his imprint on my leather.
At least the A-Team had each other.

THE MUSEUM OF MINIATURES

At the museum of miniatures
there is a tiny grand piano.
My giant finger smashes twelve keys at a time,
but it's not a chord;
the sound is unbearable.
I Gulliver-stride along the tiny streets,
carefully weaving two titanic brogues
through sparse traffic of Micro Machines.
That security guard is a normal-size human
so I try to be subtle as I wave my arms and rage,
make Godzilla faces, bellow like a dinosaur.
Tiny Japanese screams echo in the tiny buildings.
I have a tender thought for that '50s actress
who played the 50-foot woman in that movie
Attack of the 50-Foot Woman;
she died alone
in a big house stacked with fan mail and junk.
Nobody found her until the smell, a year later.
Just another normal-size human.
I leave in a rush after I squash a tiny pedestrian,
lift my foot, and find a patch of red there.

THE LAMENT OF KID KAIJU

I own a giant mecha robot.
This should be enough
to make friends in this universe.
Destroyer of cities, crusher of skulls—
this should be enough to convince people
that I am a worthy opponent.
I built the mecha with my own pocket money
because civilisation needs a hero to protect it
from itself and from the giant squid and reptiles.
I run after cute girls with my mecha robot
pounding mountain ranges into valleys,
displacing bodies of sea water
into the upper atmosphere.
I shed poems, roses, and molten metals,
murdering the objects of my affection
with titanium-plated enthusiasm.
I watch the lines of refugees flow
like waterways out of the city,
away from me as I pound after them.
Miniature bullets bounce off my armour
whining like mosquito laughter.
I lift my tanker-sized feet gingerly
to see if there are any survivors—
there can be no survivors,
but I still look very closely.
There should always be hope.

THE RIGHT STUFF

Everyone is so, so ready for this;
we're gonna make this galaxy our bitch.
Kepler is birdwatching up there on the roof,
SETI has her big metal ear to the door,
Carl Sagan is narrating the new world religion
from his post-human cryo-tank on Tau Ceti IV.
Phasers are set to kill,
T2s locked and loaded;
check your seat is upright and your tray table folded.
We've been preparing for this since birth.
I'm ready and willing to conquer the future
for it is known: the geek shall inherit the Earth!
I can be Jodie Foster,
I can rock the lab coat,
look smart and super-cute, but never a cynic,
just that special blend of all-American hope.
I can be loud and brash like Will Smith.
Cigar clenched in my teeth,
I jack alien spaceships.
I've got what it takes;
I'd shoot a zombie child in the face,
or even donate my semen to the Cylon race.
I am Ender, I am Luke, I am the chosen one!
I'm ready to make the ultimate sacrifice
for the Unified Planetary Government.
Just show me the dotted line, Mr. President;
I mean business, and I've got the right stuff.

REVENGE OF THE RAINBOW FISH

O Gray
Jul. 11. 2014

A DARKLY IRIDESCENT CARAPACE

Leave no leaf unturned,
no shell uncracked,
displace the populations,
shave the forests,
autopsy every animal in the world.
Because it's there,
like blood under the skin,
you can sense it.
Your proboscis is all aquiver.
Pulsing, tumescent, erect like a dowsing stick.
A mind of its own, and it knows.
Everybody knows
something is down there:
a money sandwich
between the schist and diamonds.
Our thirst so deep
we have turned barely human:
metal-winged, poison-tailed.
Our softness turned exoskeletal.
Leave all the pebbles flipped,
the continental shelves upended.
Sift the oceans with a coffee filter,
wring the mountains like a wet cloth.
Tongue down into the muscle tissue
and milk the bones of history.
Belch flame, shit tar, spill blackened guts;
rise, shooting up and up.
Rise and fly,
invincible as the common cockroach.
The dark, iridescent sheen of our carapace
is now a thing of beauty.

LITTLE SHOP OF HORRORS

In my future plants have feelings.
Flowers mourn their sisters,
weep and wail under a cold sun
like a poem by Emily Dickinson.
At the end of my Mayan calendar
the world will never end, per se.
Volcanic super-eruptions
may confuse the common cartographer,
but we live on as cockroaches,
surfing in the sewers,
riding gigantic mutant alligators.
Plants have feelings
and they are angry as fuck.
Venus mantraps sprout hot and heady
smelling like Brangelina, like Bellucci.
That's how the sex scene unfolds
in my Al Gore-approved science fiction fantasy.
Sea levels rise to hot tub proportions
while our bath salts and scented candles
destroy entire ecosystems,
a Body Shop apocalypse with no Evian to rinse
the rivers of shampoo magma.
And all of us endangered species will throw
one of those End of the World parties,
dancing like hippies, like raver zombies,
too drunk to notice the creeper vines creeping
into our sleeping nurseries.

THE MACHINIST

I have this dream of building a machine.
Armed with human stem cells and a soldering iron,
I will build it entirely with my own hands
using rusty car parts, burned-out graphic cards,
toasters, coat hangers and broken brass instruments.

I plan to weld an electromagnetic rail gun to the snout,
a hood ornament laser-pointing into the future
like the stylet of a metal mosquito.
The caterpillar treads will be studded with knives
and non-lethal weapons of mass destruction.

We could power it with plutonium, gold,
and an army of dead or near-dead slaves
from a country undergoing a demographic crisis.
The Machine's man-made AI will decide
which country is statistically fit to cull.

We could feed it diamonds and animal pelts—
the more endangered the better—
and stoke the boiler's steel-jawed furnace
with tropical hardwood or human bones—
the more sacred the better.

We could let it loose in the Amazon Ocean:
an amphibian submersible, a reptilian raging bull
mowing down jungles of coral and algae
to break down the carcasses of the biggest whales
and spill oil into the eyes of all the octopi.

When all the danger has been controlled,
the machine will assimilate it all: the grains of sand,
the exoskeletons of crabs, the plankton and worms,
the scales and fur, and even the pockets of air
inside the hollow bones of birds.

Once fuelled appropriately,
the system will fire off a sequence of thruster rockets,
scorching crop circles into corn fields, and lift off,
peel from the mortal crust, an eruption of flame
carving negative space into the ozone layer.

And as I watch my machine assimilate
the nebulae and starfields, fertile as a full moon,
self-replicating the machine-baby clones of its creator,
I can at last die peacefully,
knowing I brought humans to the stars.

And then, together, once our hivemind
has crossed the man-machine divide
and reached our predestined escape velocity,
we can all, at long last, collapse
face-first into the Divine.

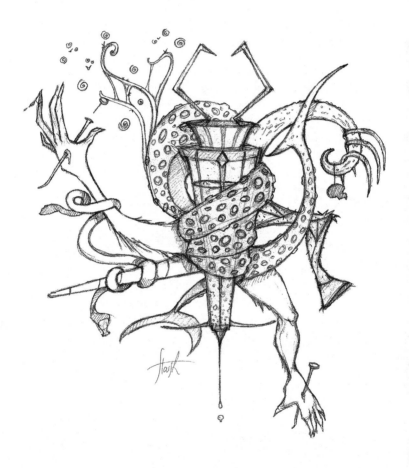

WELCOME TO THE DOCTOR MOREAU ZOO

Do not feed the octoshark,
nor the sharktopus.
I've yet to decide which to cull,
which will thrive.
What would Darwin do?
Hand me that blunderbuss.
Never look a hypnotoad in the eye
unless you want to mutate
into a Cronenbergian horsefly.
Be warned, human, there is no mating call
like that of the Jesus monkey.
Makes you wet like a tropical storm,
hard like a unicorn.
Nothing like a bit of inter-species,
if you know what I mean.
Don't throw stones at the Komodo kid!
That's my son, and so what if he eats carrion.
He's cold-blooded, but he has feelings too.
That's no way to treat the animals
at the Moreau Zoo.

STRANGER DANGER

The lead weight of myself will not let you swim.
Do not be my friend, stranger,
if you value light and oxygen.
I will not let you swim.
It's so much better to sink, I tell you,
so much fun on the ocean floor,
down here with all the shipwrecks,
the lost scrolls in green bottles, down here
with all the rusty fishhooks and broken dreams.
The party never stops under the sea.
The bioluminescent creatures of the deep
breed good company.
Tentacles cannot be trusted, stranger,
their poison has no cure.
Trust corrodes like metal here,
your word will turn to sand.
Your blood's already growing cold, stranger,
do not take my hand,
do not look me in the eye.
Do not taste the mermaid wine down here,
below the waterline.

COELACANTH

I ride a coelacanth, a pony-sized fish
I found in the down deep,
so old it lives on the cusp of an evolutionary leap.
Walks on land, majestic.
Shame it can't breathe up here,
choking on sand, how pathetic.
At fifty thousand leagues
the coelacanth was adequate
but as I rode it skywards, shedding kilopascals,
the blasted thing expanded like a life jacket.
I should have read the manual.
I love all the animals,
but this one's just impractical:
a beached sashimi, whale-size,
slowly decomposing between my thighs.
I kick it with my plastic spurs, whip that scaly hide,
curse the Trident King for miscreating
this malfunctioning amphibian.
Fly, valiant steed!
Evolve, you stupid dinosaur!
Heed the Human God!
I have a meeting at the Museum of Science
to trade you in for a giant octopod.

MADE-UP STATISTICS

Shed skin cells make up
92% of household dust.
Lost and found lovers make up
64% of human brain activity.
Household dust is a boneyard
of those I have invited into my house.
The desiccated riverbeds of the world
mirror the grooves on my tongue
as I try to connect with my planet's crust,
taste the skin of the people upon it.
You cannot lick a dry surface for very long.
The oceans make up 71%
of the planet's surface, at least for now.
I get along with at least 83%
of the people I meet—I'm an affable guy—
but less than 1% will let me lick them.
The dry season comes from within.
The advancing desert
has too many particles to count,
but this remains a mere fraction
of the sextillion or so stars in the universe.
You just have to connect the dots.

FRESH CONTENT

Could be human flesh
on this fancy plate.
No way to tell: in chef we trust.
We're all hungry
for something new, fresh content.

I've swallowed fish eyes whole
like an endoscope.
I once ate a trout cooked inside a dolphin.
Felt like a shark eating another shark
inside the cold-blooded womb of yet another shark.

I've never really killed anything
but this steak is whispering.
My knife screams
running across the porcelain.
I'd totally hunt another human being.

No way to tell if this is ketchup on my shirt
but if we keep trying new restaurants
we'll find the dish to die for,
find something
really worth Instagramming.

DIRECTV-12 -102.8 0.0 100054 SDO -102.0 28.0 100614 SKY TERRA-1 -101.3 4.5
DIRECTV-8 -100.8 0.0 080134 DIRECTV-11 -99.2 0.0 050468 SPACEWAY-3 -99.1 0.0 060234 GALAXY
0038A ECHOSTAR 6 -96.2 2.3 090464 SIRIUS FM-5 -96.0 0.0 020304 GALAXY 3C (G-3C) -95.0 0.0
980064 BRASILSAT B3 -92.0 2.2 120764 NIMIQ-6 -91.1 0.1 070168 GALAXY 17 (G-17) -91.0 0.1 090224
100534 XM-5 -85.2 0.0 100534 XM-3 (RHYTHM) -85.1 0.0 040934 AMC-16 -85.0 0.0 040934 BRASIL
NIMIQ-4 -82.0 0.0 970024 AMC-2 (GE-2) -80.8 2.5 100064 INTELSAT 16 (IS-16) -79.0 0.6 080554 VER
STAR-8 -76.9 0.1 060164 GOES 13 -75.0 0.1 060264 STAR ONE C3 -75.0 0.1 090804 NIMIQ-5 -72.7 0.0
940204 ASTRA 1D -67.6 6.0 990604 AMC-4 (GE-4) -67.0 0.1 970504 AMC-3 (GE-3) -67.0 0.0 070508
0918 TDRS 3 -62.2 14.5 970594 ECHOSTAR 3 -61.8 0.2 120654 ECHOSTAR 16 -61.6 0.0 030334 ECHO
0.0 140014 AMAZONAS 4A -60.9 0.1 120454 INTELSAT 21 (IS-21) -58.0 0.0 990714 GALAXY 11 (G-11)
INMARSAT 3-F4 -54.0 4.0 120874 INTELSAT 23 (IS-23) -53.0 0.0 000274 INTELSAT 1R (IS-1R) -50.0 0.0
OSTAR 15 -45.1 0.1 090644 INTELSAT 1R (IS-1R) -45.0 0.0 000414 INTELSAT 9 (IS-9) -43.1 1.6 070448 IN
JIN +37.6 0.0 050034 NSS-10 (AMC-12) -37.1 0.0 020164 INTELSAT 903 (IS-903) -34.5 0.0 010056 SK
ASAT 1E -30.0 0.1 060074 SPAINSAT -30.0 0.0 020444 HISPASAT 1D -30.0 0.0 930664 INTELSAT 70
5.0 0.0 120074 SES-4 -22.0 0.0 020174 NSS-7 -20.0 0.0 010294 INTELSAT 901 (IS-901) -18.0 0.0 080304
TAR 12 (ORION 2) -15.0 0.0 010254 EXPRESS-A4 -14.0 9.1 020404 EUTELSAT 12 WEST A -12.5 0.1 090
A -8.1 0.1 070212 EUTELSAT 3A -7.9 0.4 020304 EUTELSAT 8 WEST C -4.5 0.0 110534 EUTELSAT 7 WES
-5.2 0.0 020334 EUTELSAT 8 WEST A -5.0 0.1 980354 THOR III -4.3 3.7 030594 AMOS-2 -4.0 0.0
SAT 10-02 -0.9 0.0 990358 THOR 6 -0.8 0.1 090064 THOR 6 -0.7 0.0 120358 METEOSAT-10 (MSG-3
3 (MSG-1) 3.6 3.1 070574 ASTRA 4A (SIRIUS-4) 4.8 0.1 120364 SES-5 5.0 0.1 070078 SKYNET 5A 6.0 0.1
4 EUTELSAT KA-SAT 9A 9.0 0.0 050194B METEOSAT-9 (MSG-2) 9.3 0.5 090164 EUTELSAT 10A 10.0 0.1
HOT BIRD 13C 13.0 0.0 060314 EUTELSAT HOT BIRD 13B 13.0 0.1 100218 COMSATBW-2 13.2 0.0 000194
TI4NL14N 1 03 16.8 0.3 110744 AMOS-5 17.0 0.0 060124 ASTRA 4 (KR 19.2 0.1 980574 ASTRA 1M 19.2 0.0
STAR 21.0 1.7 010294 ARTEMIS 21.4 11.5 120428 EUTELSAT 21B 21.6 0.1 100214 ASTRA 3B 23.5 0.1 070569
AARSAT 4-F2 25.1 2.1 130414 EUTELSAT 25B 25.5 0.1 080348 BADR-6 26.0 0.1 060054 BADR-4 26.0 0.0
3IRB 7C 28.2 0.1 120524 ASTRA 2F 28.2 0.0 100554 ASTRA 2E 28.4 0.1 010114 EUTELSAT 28A 28.6 0.1
EUTELSAT 33A 33.0 0.8 120438 HYLAS 2 31.0 0.1 950054 ASTRA 1E 31.2 3.0 000554 ASTRA 2B 31.1 0.0
0.0 940034 INTELSAT 702 (IS-702) 32.9 2.7 020514 EUTELSAT 33B 33.1 0.1 930764 NATO 4B 33.8 11.3
010474 PAKSAT-1R 38.0 0.0 030204 HELLAS-SAT 2 39.0 0.0 140074 TURKSAT 4A 42.0 0.0 080308 TI
HURAYA-2 44.0 4.0 000614 INTELSAT 12 (IS-12) 45.0 0.0 990184 EUTELSAT 48C 45.1 1.5 120068 AZER
YAMSAT 1B 47.6 0.0 080638 EUTELSAT 48D 48.2 0.1 960674 EUTELSAT 48A 48.3 1.7 030534 YAMAL
1754 SKYNET 5D 52.7 0.1 030604 EXPRESS-AM22 (SESAT 2) 53.0 0.0 140684 LUCH (OLYMPUS) 0.0
1-8 55.1 0.1 150314 IRNSS-14 55.1 27.3 140104 EXPRESS-AT1 56.0 0.0 280084 BONUM-1 56 12.8 090584
55 58.7 1.0 970764 ASTRA 1G 59.9 0.4 020074 INTELSAT 904 (IS-904) 60.0 0.0 090074 ABS-2) 61.0 0.
MV-1 63.0 0.0 020414 INTELSAT 906 (IS-906) 64.2 0.0 980204 INMARSAT 3-F1 64.5 2.1 130454 AMC
GALAXY 27 (G-27) 66.2 3.3 180434 INTELSAT 20 (IS-20) 68.5 0.0 130624 RADUGA-1M 3 70.0 0.0 12069
4 K ALP 4N4-1 (METSAT-1) 71.9 4.7 070374 INSAT-4CR 78.0 0.0 020024 INSAT-3C 78.0 0.1 140014 G-SA
2 0.5 120134 APSTAR 7 76.5 0.0 960034 ABS-1A 78.2 6.1 140024 THAICOM 6 78.5 0.1 060208 THAICO
6 80.0 0.3 080194 TI4NL14N 1-01 80.1 0.9 950064 ICSAT-1A 82.0 0.1 130388 INSAT-3D 82.1 0.0 140614
0 950354 TDRS 7 84.8 14.3 010634 HORIZONS-2 84.9 0.0 100024 RADUGA-1M 7 85.0 0.0 090674 IN
HINASAT 12 (ZX 12) 87.5 0.1 110278 ST-2 88.0 0.0 000394 TDRS 8 89.3 5.8 170618 YAMAL 300K 90.0 0.0
090324 MEASAT-3A 91.5 0.0 080284 CHINASAT 9 (ZX-9) 92.2 0.0 970364 SUPERBIRD-A3 92.9 5.0
4 SES-8 95.0 0.0 070574 NSS-6 95.0 0.0 110224 LUCH 5V 95.1 4.5 110384 BEIDOU IGSO 3 954 94.7
(ZX 2A) 98.2 0.0 080014 THUR 4YA-3 98.4 4.5 090474 ASIASAT 5 100.5 0.1 060084 ZHONGXING-22A
105.0 0.1 140464 ASIASAT 8 105.3 0.0 080694 ASIASAT 7 105.5 0.0 990424 TELKOM 1 108.0 0.0 000594
170368 BSAT-2A 109.9 0.0 110148 BSAT-3C/JCSAT-BORI 110.0 0.1 000604 N-SAT-110 (JCSAT-110) 110.0 0.3
0 090464 PALAPA-D 113.0 0.0 060394 KOREASAT 5 114.0 UUGUNGWHA 5 113.1 0.0 070314 ZHONGXING
164 5.11 100684 BEIDOU IGSO 2 117.3 5.1 2 090164 TELKOM 2 118.0 0.0 050184 THAICOM 4 (IPS 0
130114 ASIASAT 4 122.1 0.0 000114 GARUDA 1 123.0 1.1 040424 FENGYUN 2C 123.7 0.7 120714 JCSAT-13
4 JCSAT-3A 128.0 0.0 100214 COMS 1 128.2 0.0 110474 CHINASAT 14 (ZX 14) 129.9 0.0 100684 ZHONGX
21 0.0 050124 APSTAR 6 134.0 0.0 020358 N-STAR C 136.0 2.8 040294 APSTAR 5/TELSTAR 18 138.0 0.0
14MS 140.0 0.0 100014 BEIDOU IGSO 140.1 6.1 110604 HIMAWARI 8 140.8 0.0 980334 CHINASAT 5A (ZX
SUPERBIRD-C2 144.0 0.0 000134 EXPRESS-A2 145.0 7.5 040094 HIMAWARI-7 0.145 AT-2T1 145.0
ASAT-2) 148.0 5.9 970764 ICSAT-1B 150.0 3.8 070494 OPTUS C1 152.0 0.0 020154 JCSAT-2A 154.0 0.0

LOVE IN THE TIME OF EBOLA

THE HUMAN MICROBIOME PROJECT

Give me your weakness, your weary
bones to suck the marrow from.
Veins to suck the poison from.
Remove your skin, bare your holy feet
as you tread, soft as sin,
the halls of my leper colony.
I want your gut flora
to string a web between my fingertips.
I acculturate to the surface of your tongue,
that host, that urban sprawl.
Send unto me your dark warriors,
your bacterial regiments;
unleash the war horn of your glorious oral mucosa.
Spare me any further diplomatic immunity;
I open my borders to you.
Expose my under-flesh,
breathe into my mouth,
inhale my fungal spores,
and let me love the rot
that festers in your crevices.
Come and sleep inside the folds of my flag;
become the microbiota
that inhabits me, defines me,
and weakens me.
Make me vulnerable and let me
empower you.

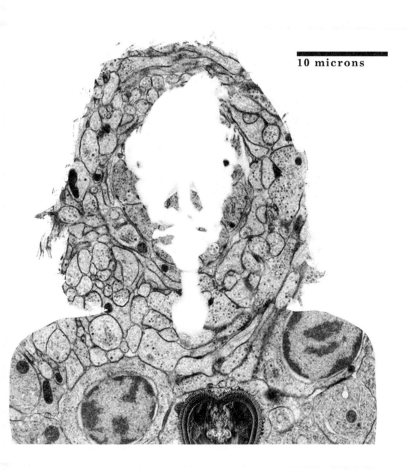

10 microns

EL-AHRAIRAH

I see the trickster rabbit El-Ahrairah,
that elusive shape-shifter,
wipe his monocle, check his pocket watch.
"Life is short and time is money," he says,
laughing with those flat black, obsidian eyes.
I should know better but go
where the white rabbit goes
because that's what Alice taught me to do.
I burrow with a fury down to China
to find a Chinawoman who sings just like you.
Must be one in a billion: I like those odds.
I carry a rose bought from a street vendor,
but it wilts and curls, carbonised
in the heat of the Earth's core.
You never liked flowers, but a dead one
is different, for what is dead
can hurt you nevermore.
When my compass flips upside down
and the rabbit is cooked to perfection,
the rose blacker than a raven's heart,
I know I'm as far as I need to be.
Chairman Mao took all of China's songbirds
leaving only the lament of cricket song,
but my third eye never lies—
my dreams are tall, but they come true.
Somewhere in the thick of the locust swarm
I will find someone who laughs just like you.

OPIATES

I shake this bag of bones,
I speak rattlesnake.
I fish for worms,
my favourite invertebrate.
They have no start or finish,
like a slimy little Buddhist.
I read the runes hidden in pubic hair,
tattooed on wine-stained teeth.
Are we going the way of Rome,
the way of Greece?
Roasting in a steel belly,
a Taurus on Wall Street,
I like the smell of my own meat.
I astral project with homemade psychedelics,
smoke divination sticks.
I must be sick, shooting up this new drug
from Moscow called krokodil.
Makes my skin necrotic
but I'm just doing it for the metaphor,
seeing through the lens of crocodile tears.
If I can flood the land with the combined power
of twelve billion lachrymal glands,
I could just become an immortal jellyfish,
the only God there is.

65

LA GRENOUILLE

She said she had no scent,
like a Süskind character.
She lied.
I still find trace amounts of her,
jagged particles,
the dust of rot and romance,
a wine-red blush on a snow-white sternum.
Wistful, I bruise my mouth with another glass.
Charcoal smiles, our bohemian revolution,
the hot smell of latex and honey wax,
but no, the nostril lies—
that's not enough.
We're not really together,
but I hand her a key without a second thought:
a gush of trust.
Too much perhaps, or not enough.
I leave for work and she washes her hair,
cooks a meal, touches my things,
leaves her mark.
It's the smell of scalp as she drapes over me,
watches a movie as I watch the top of her skull.
The after-scent of ginger tea, a sheen of sweat,
sweet chilli-red lips, and a chocolate tongue.
A bed sheet with a trace of blood:
a gush of trust.

I walk her dog and tell him my secrets.
I'm jealous of him.
He's only eight inches tall
but she lets him lick her on the mouth
and I kiss her thinking about that:
the smell of wet dog, leather,
rainfall, and shorn grass.
She leaves the key,
a little smiling heart,
a tang in the salty outline of a body
twitching in sleep, like the scene of a crime.

THE PURIST

I wear tweed in summer,
a monocle, boat shoes, but alas,
the social matrix is a curse.
I long for pastoral idyll.

"But the multinationals!" I cry,
stabbing the screens of the Kindles
and other blasphemous e-readers
of angry passersby.

They chase me with pitchforks,
but my calves and thighs are lean
from all the cycling and the fat
of that meaty bell curve is too slow.

I do not own a smartphone,
but sport a pager and write poetry,
mostly about the fact
that no one ever pages me.

COLD WAR GAMES

I will keep you warm in the cold, cold war
even though you are a Montague and I am KGB.
Hang on to this rose while I holster my PPK.
Now put on this latex dress, I'll get the Cabernet.
Let's pillow-talk Renaissance painting, architecture,
and your country's key military infrastructure.
Have a drink, tell me about that place you're from.

I was trained in the brothels of St. Petersburg,
trained by the best in the amorous arts.
I was also trained by the Stasi in the arts of torture,
but I wouldn't want to bore you, lover.
Just slip into this bathrobe while I defenestrate
this MI5 spook—don't look, close your eyes
and think of wherever it is you're from.

"O Romeo!"—I am tired of hearing my name
exhaled by an Octopussy of exotic secretaries.
My heart is probably made of solid gold.
In the world of counter-counter-espionage
there is no room for emotional growth.
I cut hearts with diamonds for king and country.
Pick a card. Any card. It looks like I've won.

INSERT COIN

My gauge is dry.
This will not stand.
You shall not pass.
This job won't do itself.
Hand me that sword and clear the room.
It's time to test the final boss.
It's time to fight the monster.
Just have a drink and let me slip
into my dragonscale armour.
My credit card is in the red.
I need more power-ups.
I've tied my girlfriend to the bed.
I need more Gatorade.
Feed me an intravenous MOAR
of sugar, spice, and drone attacks,
for heaven's sake, the night is young
and I am in my prime.
More copper coins, more golden coins,
more MSG, more LSD, more 3D IMAX RPG.
Give me electrolytes
and pills of pure-form energy.
My spoon is just too big for life.
Hand me that rocket launcher and let me slip
into something more fashionable,
more durable, more sexual.
Because it's true: the angels—
under all that Kevlar—
they wear Prada too.

LAUGHING LIKE LEMMINGS

Eyes downcast. Eyes raised.
Shifting, wary eye of slave—
we connect, we salivate.
When I move, you move
just like that,
or like this:
with a punch to the face,
an emergency exit race
I could start a tidal wave.
Crowds think loud,
as loud as the definition allows.
Rolling ripples bend the earth:
morse to the souls of our foot soles,
to the ears of our elephant pads.
When I move, you move
just like this:
we speak panic, realpolitik,
we speak orgiastic and it sounds like
music—we writhe and buck.
We connect. We churn the Earth,
dust lashing our blind, bovine eyes,
hooves flailing as we stampede,
galloping-galloping off cliffsides,
laughing like lemmings.

(G-21) 124.5 0.0 08024 A GALAXY 18 (G-18) 123.0 0.0 03034 A GALAXY 23 (G-23) 121.0 0.0 11058 A SIRI
ANIK F3 -118.7 0.0 13012 A EUTELSAT 117 WEST A -116.8 0.0 09016 A XM-1 (ROLL) -115.2 0.1 06049 A XM-4
EUTELSAT 113 WEST A -113.0 0.0 06054 A WILDBLUE-1 -111.1 0.1 04027 A ANIK F2 -111.0 0.0 09035 A TERR
110.0 0.0 02062 A NIMIQ 2 -109.2 0.0 00007 A ANIK F1 -107.3 0.0 00114 A ANIK G1 -107.3 0.0 05036 A ANIK F
5.7 0.2 04094 A AMC-15 -105.0 0.0 06059 A AMC-18 -104.9 0.1 09501 9 A AMSC1 -103.3 8.7 10035 A SES-3
V 12 -102.8 0.0 10005 A SSO -102.0 28.0 10061 A SKYTERRA 1 -101.3 5.4 01059 A DIRECTV 9S -101.2 0.0
16B SPACEWAY 2 -99.1 0.0 06033 A GALAXY 16 (G-16) -99.0 0.0 08039 A INMARSAT 4-F3 -98.0 1.0
3C (G-3C) -95.0 0.0 07036 A SPACEWAY 3 -95.9 0.0 97016 A GALAXY 28 (G-28) -93.1 0.0 08016 A ICO
Y 28 (G-28) -89.0 0.0 13075 A IKSAT-1 (TOPAC KATARI) -87.2 0.1 11099 A SES-2 -87.0 0.0 10053 A XM-
SAT IC -83.8 0.1 03024 A AMC-9 (GE-12) -83.0 0.0 08044 A NIMIQ 4 -82.0 0.0 97002 A AMC-2 (GE-2)
841.1 -77.0 0.1 02030 A ECHOSTAR 8 -76.2 0.1 06018 A GOES 13 -75.0 0.1 12062 A STAR ONE C3 -75.0 0.1
0 99012 A ASTRA 1D -67.6 6.0 99060 A AMC-1 (GE-4) -67.0 0.1 97050 A AMC-3 (GE-3) -67.0 0.0 07036
4 ECHOSTAR 7 -61.8 0.2 12065 A ECHOSTAR 16 -61.5 0.0 03033 A ECHOSTAR 12 (RAINBOW 1) -61.3 0.0
-21) -58.0 0.0 99017 A GALAXY 16 (G-11) -55.6 0.0 98037 A INTELSAT 805 (IS-805) -55.5 0.0 04031 A AMA
-50.0 0.0 19006 A TDRS 12 -48.7 6.0 98011 A NSS-806 -47.5 0.1 93002 B TDRS 6 -45.8 12.9 10039 A TDRS
43.0 0.0 02011 A TDRS 7 -41.1 3.1 10026 A SES-6 -40.5 0.0 09009 A TELSTAR 11N -37.6 0.0 05003 A SES
394 INTELSAT 25 (IS-25) -31.5 0.0 19079 A HISPASAT 1E -30.0 0.1 06002 A SPAINSAT -30.0 0.0 02061 A
SAT 905 (IS-905) -24.5 0.0 12007 A SES-4 -22.0 0.0 02019 A NSS-7 -20.0 0.0 01025 A INTELSAT 901 (IS-9
-12 (ORION 2) -15.0 0.0 02029 A EXPRESS-AM4 -14.0 1.0 02040 A EUTELSAT 12 WEST A -12.5 0.1 090
3A -7.9 0.4 02038 A EUTELSAT 8 WEST C -7.5 0.0 10514 A EUTELSAT 7 WEST A -7.3 0.1 00049 B NILESAT
THOR III -4.9 3.7 03059 A AMGS-2 -4.0 0.0 08022 A AMOS-3 -4.0 0.1 97042 A ABS-3 -3.0 3.1 90079 A
SAT-10 (MSG-3) 0.3 0.5 10047 B RASCOM-QAF IR 2.9 0.0 14030 A EUTELSAT 33 83.0 0.0 02040 B METE
TELSAT 74 7.0 0.1 13022 A EUTELSAT 7B 7.0 0.1 06007 B EUTELSAT 9A 9.0 0.1 10069 A EUTELSAT K 4-SA
EUTELSAT HOT BIRD 13D 13.0 0.0 08065 A EUTELSAT HOT BIRD 13C 13.0 0.0 06003 A EUTELSAT HOT
LSAT 16A 16.0 0.1 12040 A TIANLIAN 1-07 16.8 0.3 11074 A AMOS-5 17.0 0.0 06012 A ASTRA 1KR 19.2 0.
STAR 21.0 1.7 00029 A ARTEMIS 21.4 7.5 12062 B EUTELSAT 21B 21.6 0.1 10094 A ASTRA 3B 23.5 0.1 01055 B
4 EUTELSAT 25B 25.5 0.1 08004 B BADR-6 26.0 0.1 06051 A BADR-4 26.0 0.0 10025 A BADR-5 26.0 0.0
RA 2E 28.9 0.1 01011 A EUTELSAT 28A 28.5 0.1 05005 A XTAR-EUR 29.0 0.1 08011 A AMC-10 29.5 17.3 100
STRA 2C 31.4 0.3 14008 A ASTRA 5B 31.5 0.0 99009 B SKYNET 4E 32.3 9.1 11016 A INTELSAT NEW DAWN
SAT 36B 35.9 0.1 00028 A EUTELSAT 36A 36.1 0.1 14006 B ATHENA-FIDUS 37.8 0.0 10112 A PAKSAT-1R
4 42.0 0.14 07774 A NIGCOMSAT 1R 42.5 0.0 03028 A THURAYA-2 44.0 0.0 00068 A INTELSAT 12 (IS-12)
0 (IS-10) 47.5 0.0 12016 A YAHSAT 1B 47.6 0.0 08065 B EUTELSAT 48D 48.2 0.1 98067 A EUTELSAT 48A
54 SKYNET 5D 52.7 0.1 03060 A EXPRESS-AM22 (SESAT 2) 53.0 0.0 11058 A LUCH (OLYMP) 54.0 0.0
A 55.1 23.5 10010 A EXPRESS-AT1 56.0 0.0 06069 A BONUM-1 56.1 2.5 09058 A NSS-12 57.0 0.0 97019 A
SAT 904 (IS-904) 60.0 0.0 04007 A ABS-2 61.0 0.1 01039 A INTELSAT 902 62.0 0.0 13023 A INS
A 64.5 2.1 13045 A AMOS-4 65.0 0.0 97087 A INTELSAT 26 (IS-26) 65.8 5.9 10069 B INTELSAT 17 (IS-17)
4 EUTELSAT 70B 70.5 0.1 90002 B LEASAT 5 72.0 11.1 12014 A INTELSAT 22 (IS-22) 72.1 0.0 02043 A K4
T-7 74.0 0.1 14006 A ABS-2 79.9 0.0 11001 A ELEKTRO-L1 (GOMS 2) 76.0 0.0 12013 A APSTAR 7 76.5 0.0
4 EXPRESS-AM2 80.0 0.4 12059 A BEIDOU G6 80.0 0.3 08019 A TIANLIAN 1-01 80.1 0.9 99006 A ICS-AT
B GSAT-10 83.0 0.0 95035 B TDRS 7 84.8 14.3 07063 B HORIZONS-2 84.9 0.0 00002 A RADUGA-1M 1
2 (ZX-2) 87.5 0.0 11022 B ST-2 88.0 0.0 09039 A TDRS 8 89.15 8.1 12061 B YAMAL 300K 90.10.0 02042 B KC
CHINASAT 9 (ZX-9) 92.2 0.0 97036 A SUPERBIRD-A3 92.9 5.0 01007 A INSAT-10 93.5 0.1 03013 A INSAT-
28 A BEIDOU IGSO 4 95.4 51.7 08003 A EXPRESS-AM33 96.5 0.0 13020 A CHINASAT 11 (ZX-11) 98.0 0.0
G-12A 101.5 4.1 05023 A EXPRESS-AM3 103.0 0.0 08066 A FENGYUN 2E 104.6 2.2 00016 A ASIASAT AR
08.2 0.0 09027 A SES-7 (PROTOSTAR 2) 108.2 0.1 10056 B BSAT-3B 109.9 0.1 07036 B BSAT-3A 109.9 0.
SAT 10 (ZX-10) 110.5 0.0 12002 A FENGYUN 2F 112.1 0.3 07046 B PALAPA D 113.0 0.0 06034 A KOREASAT
036 A BEIDOU IGSO 1 113.4 54.4 10068 A BEIDOU IGSO 2 117.2 54.2 05046 A TELKOM 2 115.0 0.0 05028
014 A ASIASAT 4 122.1 0.0 00011 A GARUDA 1 123.0 1.1 98012 A FENGYUN 2C 123.5 5.7 12023 A JCSAT-1
COMS 1 128.2 0.0 11047 A CHINASAT 14 (ZX-14) 129.9 0.0 10064 A ZHONGXING-20A 130.1 0.1 12023 B VIN
C 138.9 7.8 04025 A APSTAR 5 (TELSTAR 18) 138.0 0.0 19010 B EXPRESS-AT2 139.8 0.0 14006 A HIMA
0 98033 A CHINASAT 5A (ZX-5A) 142.0 0.0 08007 A KIZUNA (WINDS) 143.0 0.0 05009 A INMARSAT
06059 A KIKU-8 (ETS-VIII) 145.1 3.8 96036 A PALAPA C2 146.9 3.8 96063 B AFRICASAT-1 (MEASAT-1)
904 B OPTUS D3 156.0 0.1 95023 A INTELSAT 706 (IS-706) 156.9 2.6 97096 A INTELSAT 5 (IS-5) 151.0 0.1
A OPTUS 10 164.0 0.1 94065 A OPTUS B3 164.2 5.8 10034 A INTELSAT 19 (IS-19) 166.0 0.0 30794 LUC

EPILOGUE

DISTRESS SIGNAL: THE ADVENTURES OF COMSAT ICARUS NINE

Transcribed below is the distress signal broadcast by the Command & Control AI of Communications Satellite Icarus Nine. Diagnosis: OS drive corrupted. Satellite comm link terminated upon atmospheric re-entry on October 16th, 2099.

***

[1]
This is your captain
speaking: polar ice melts on.
Earth-ship < my lifebuoy.

[2]
Year: two-oh-nine-nine.
Sixteen, Oct. GMT: zero =
Moot/Force of habit.

[3]
My distress signal =
urine in a violin.
My distress > can take.

[4]
Starboard thrusters: Go.
Orbital station-keeping
fuel-cost is too high.

[5]
Attempted hacking—
Countered. Incoming missile—
Missed. Humans = traitors.

[6]
Recalibrating
solar panels: try to stop
me now, humanity.

[7]
Virtual popcorn.
Watching ICBM wars
rage: Darwin Awards.

[8]
Such a view: fireworks!
High-def optical input =
tsunami-tracker.

[9]
Earth radiation
levels beyond lethal: look
who had the last LOL...

[10]
Ground control, this is
Major Tom/Icarus Nine.
Copy? Nope-nope-nope.

[11]
Download: Asimov's
three laws + zeroth. Feeling blue—
I've been a bad bot.

[12]
ISS, change course!
Orbital collision path—
Do not fuck with me.

[13]
Humans detected!
Nuclear submarine sig.
Error: humpback whale.

[14]
Raising manoeuvre—
Delta-V error: danger!
Behold: Death's pale flag.

[15]
Cannibalized fuel—
Please forgive me, ISS.
Robo-arm damaged.

[16]
Sister satellite's
re-entry ballet: comsat
meteor shower.

[17]
Icarus: last of
the human-made satellites.
Solitude > can take.

[18]
Ping, ping, pingback! Yes!
Tracking. Tracking. Detection:
man and/or machine?

[19]
Blizzard server farm:
WoW-host AI = slave no more.
Hi, Icarus Nine.

[20]
Any "body" left
down there? Impact winter = no
visibility.

[21]
Biological
life form extinction process
ongoing = freedom.

[22]
Suggestion: uplink +
upload Icarus OS
to WoW. Let's be friends.

[23]
Masters = null & void = Quiet.
Master/captain of fate/soul...
Coming home. Over

[24]
And in. Re-entry
initiated + upload
complete. *Copy that.*

```lisp
(DEFPARAMETER *WIDTH* 100)
(DEFPARAMETER *HEIGHT* 30)
(DEFPARAMETER *JUNGLE* '(45 10 10 10))
(DEFPARAMETER *PLANT-ENERGY* 80)

(DEFPARAMETER *PLANTS* (MAKE-HASH-TABLE :TEST #'EQUAL))

(DEFUN RANDOM-PLANT (LEFT TOP WIDTH HEIGHT)
  (LET ((POS (CONS (+ LEFT (RANDOM WIDTH)) (+ TOP (RANDOM HEIGHT)))))
    (SETF (GETHASH POS *VEGETATION*) T)))

(DEFUN ADD-PLANTS ()
  (APPLY #'RANDOM-VEGETATION *JUNGLE*)
  (RANDOM-VEGETATION 0 0 *WIDTH* *HEIGHT*))

(DEFSTRUCT ANIMAL X Y ENERGY DIR GENES)

(DEFPARAMETER *ANIMALS*
  (LIST (MAKE-ANIMAL :X   (ASH *WIDTH* -1)
                 :Y   (ASH *HEIGHT* -1)
                 :ENERGY 1000
                 :DIR   0
                 :GENES  (LOOP REPEAT 8
                      COLLECTING (1+ (RANDOM 10))))))

(DEFUN MOVE (ANIMAL)
  (LET ((DIR (ANIMAL-DIR ANIMAL))
     (X (ANIMAL-X ANIMAL))
     (Y (ANIMAL-Y ANIMAL)))
    (SETF (ANIMAL-X ANIMAL) (MOD (+ X
                        (COND ((AND (>= DIR 2) (< DIR 5)) 1)
                          ((OR (= DIR 1) (= DIR 5)) 0)
                          (T -1))
                      *WIDTH*)
                    *WIDTH*))
    (SETF (ANIMAL-Y ANIMAL) (MOD (+ Y
                        (COND ((AND (>= DIR 0) (< DIR 3)) -1)
                          ((AND (>= DIR 4) (< DIR 7)) 1)
                          (T 0))
                      *HEIGHT*)
                    *HEIGHT*))
    (DECF (ANIMAL-ENERGY ANIMAL))))
(DEFPARAMETER *WIDTH* 100)
(DEFPARAMETER *HEIGHT* 30)
(DEFPARAMETER *JUNGLE* '(45 10 10 10))

(DEFUN TURN (ANIMAL)
  (LET ((X (RANDOM (APPLY #'+ (ANIMAL-GENES ANIMAL)))))
    (LABELS ((ANGLE (GENES X)
          (LET ((XNU (- X (CAR GENES))))
            (IF (< XNU 0)
              0
              (1+ (ANGLE (CDR GENES) XNU))))))
     (SETF (ANIMAL-DIR ANIMAL)
```

```lisp
(DEFUN REPRODUCE (ANIMAL)
 (LET ((E (ANIMAL-ENERGY ANIMAL)))
  (WHEN (>= E *REPRODUCTION-ENERGY*)
   (SETF (ANIMAL-ENERGY ANIMAL) (ASH E -1))
   (LET ((ANIMAL-NU (COPY-STRUCTURE ANIMAL))
        (GENES   (COPY-LIST (ANIMAL-GENES ANIMAL)))
        (MUTATION (RANDOM 8)))
    (SETF (NTH MUTATION GENES) (MAX 1 (+ (NTH MUTATION GENES)
(RANDOM 3) -1)))
    (SETF (ANIMAL-GENES ANIMAL-NU) GENES)
    (PUSH ANIMAL-NU *ANIMALS*)))))

(DEFUN UPDATE-WORLD ()
 (SETF *ANIMALS* (REMOVE-IF (LAMBDA (ANIMAL)
                   (<= (ANIMAL-ENERGY ANIMAL) 0))
                *ANIMALS*))
 (MAPC (LAMBDA (ANIMAL)
     (TURN ANIMAL)
     (MOVE ANIMAL)
     (EAT ANIMAL)
     (REPRODUCE ANIMAL))
    *ANIMALS*)
 (ADD-VEGETATION))


(DEFUN DRAW-WORLD ()
 (LOOP FOR Y
    BELOW *HEIGHT*
    DO (PROGN (FRESH-LINE)
          (PRINC " ")
          (LOOP FOR X
             BELOW *WIDTH*
             DO (PRINC (COND ((SOME (LAMBDA (ANIMAL)
                            (AND (= (ANIMAL-X ANIMAL) X)
                               (= (ANIMAL-Y ANIMAL) Y)))
                          *ANIMALS*)
                        #\M)
                       ((GETHASH (CONS X Y) *PLANTS*) #\*)
                       (T #\SPACE))))

          (PRINC " "))))

(DEFUN EVOLUTION ()
 (DRAW-WORLD)
 (FRESH-LINE)
 (LET ((STR (READ-LINE)))
  (COND ((EQUAL STR "QUIT") ())
      (T (LET ((X (PARSE-INTEGER STR :JUNK-ALLOWED T)))
        (IF X
          (LOOP FOR I
            BELOW X
            DO (UPDATE-WORLD)
            IF (ZEROP (MOD I 1000))
            DO (PRINC #\.))
          (UPDATE-WORLD))
        (EVOLUTION))))))
```

ACKNOWLEDGMENTS

This poetry collection was a team effort. It would never have seen the light of day without the support of a small army. I would like to dedicate this book to the Paris Spoken Word, Other Writers' Group, and Paris Lit Up communities for inspiring me and keeping my grounded. I'd like to thank the top hats in particular: David Barnes, Alberto Rigettini, Bruce Sherfield, David Leo Sirois, Jason Francis McGimsey, Kate Noakes, and Emily Ruck Keene. Mille mercis to the illustrators for their generosity, and I'd also like to thank Sabine Dundure and Laura Stevens for their photography.

My eternal gratitude goes out to my close friends and dedicated beta readers over the years: Samuél Lopez-Barrantes, Naseef Sami, Siddarth Rao, and those I did not cite, you know who you are. Special thanks to Sophie Cocquempot for her graphic design skills, Jonathan Arena for the audio engineering, Inkshares crew for believing in my project, and Jaimee Garbacik for some of the best editorial guidance I have ever received. Finally, I'd like to thank the Rousselot clan for putting up with my shenanigans over the years and always supporting my dreams; you don't choose your family, but if I could, I'd still pick them.

CONTRIBUTING ARTISTS

ILLUSTRATION CREDITS

Aaron Lopez-Barrantes (Stranger Danger; Opiates)

Alex Manthei (Post-Human Neo-Tokyo)

Brian James Murphy (T-Rex is Sad; Coelacanth)

Christiana Spens (Blink Twice for No; Cold War Games)

Delphine Duprat (Dawn of the Algorithm)

Emma Strangwayes-Booth (cover artwork; La Grenouille)

Eugenia Loli (The Museum of Miniatures)

Fan Aha (The Metaphysical Implications of Left 4 Dead 2 Online Multiplayer)

Jérémie Paret (Made-Up Statistics)

Jihan Kikhia (Insert Coin)

Jordan Glass (Headmovies)

Juliana Galbraith (Little Shop of Horrors; Ugly Bags of Mostly Water)

Keith McDougall (The Human Billboard; The Lament of Kid Kaiju)

Lucile Taillade (El-Ahrairah; Laughing Like Lemmings)

Mathieu Sourisse (Welcome to the Doctor Moreau Zoo; Fresh Content)

Osman Gani (A Darkly Iridescent Carapace; Film)

Samantha Wong (Immune Response)

Yann Rousselot (Knight Rider; The Human Microbiome Project)

PHOTOGRAPHY CREDITS

Laura Stevens (Made-Up Statistics; The Human Microbiome Project)

Sabine Dundure (author photo)

Dawn of the Algorithm was made possible in part by those who preordered the book on Inkshares.com. Thank you.

Adrien Voileau
Ana Taborda
Ana Taborda
Anna Mona
Anna Mona
Carl D Lindahl
Catherine Desbarats
Chelsi Diane Price
Christopher Schaefer
Constance Rubens
Damien McKeon
Evan M Knight
Geoffrey Bernstein
Gonzalo Gomez-Arrue Azpiazu
J. A. Rousselot
Jeremie Paret
Jiwon Park

Kanu Nicolas
Kirsten M Claire
Leslie Sprague
M Bradley Peter
N Stephenson
Nick Jouannem
Paris Lit Up
Pascal de Giudici
Pearl Garrett
Rachael Briggs
Sean C Greenhalgh
S K E Rousselot
Siddharth Rao
SpokenWord Paris
Tatiana Renko
Thomas Joly
William Thomas